IMAGES OF ASIA

Peking Opera

Series Editors, China Titles:
NIGEL CAMERON, SYLVIA FRASER-LU

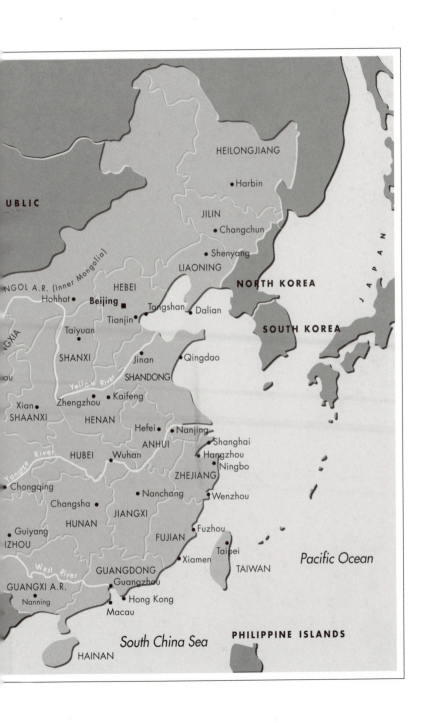

Peking Opera

COLIN MACKERRAS

HONG KONG
OXFORD UNIVERSITY PRESS
OXFORD NEW YORK
1997

Oxford University Press

Oxford New York
Athens Auckland Bangkok Bogota
Bombay Buenos Aires Calcutta Cape Town
Dar es Salaam Delhi Florence Hong Kong Istanbul
Karachi Kuala Lumpur Madras Madrid Melbourne
Mexico City Nairobi Paris Singapore
Taipei Tokyo Toronto

and associated companies in
Berlin Ibadan

Oxford is a trade mark of Oxford University Press

First published 1997
This impression (lowest digit)
1 3 5 7 9 10 8 6 4 2

Published in the United States
by Oxford University Press, New York

British Library Cataloguing in Publication Data
available

Library of Congress Cataloging-in-Publication Data

Mackerras,Colin.
Peking opera / Colin Mackerras.
p.   cm. — (Images of Asia)
Includes bibliographical references (p.   ) and index.
ISBN 0-19-587729-2 (alk. paper)
1. Operas, Chinese — History and criticism.   I. Title.   II Series.
ML1751. C4M32 1997
782.1'0951 — dc21   97-6887
CIP
MN

Printed in Hong Kong
Published by Oxford University Press (China) Ltd
18/F Warwick House, Taikoo Place, 979 King's Road,
Quarry Bay, Hong Kong

Contents

Preface

Peking Opera is a form of theatre rich in tradition, combining and integrating a whole range of art forms in a rare and stimulating way. While other varieties of opera pay attention to the music, singing, libretto, costumes, acting, and make-up used within them, Peking Opera stands alone in the extent to which these elements are integrated to form a unique whole. A performer who did not look the part or whose mastery of the expected movements or gestures was less than perfect could never get a job, however wonderful his or her singing voice. In Western opera we do not usually associate the gymnast or the mime artist with the singer in the same performer, yet such combinations are indeed common in Peking Opera. This style of integration makes up an art of rare beauty, aesthetically satisfying and, above all, exciting theatre.

Although Peking Opera itself is not particularly ancient, China's theatre tradition is, with India's, the oldest and most significant in Asia. Peking Opera represents the climax of the nation's rich and colourful theatre tradition, and yet it also exemplifies the tensions between the beauties of the traditional arts and the demands of the modern world. Inevitably modernity affects tradition, even threatening its very survival. As the classical arts appear to lose their appeal for new generations, should authorities and societies give a high priority to preserving them? Issues such as this are among the most pressing for the traditional arts in China, as they are in the rest of the contemporary world.

Peking Opera is called *jingju* or *jingxi* in Chinese, which translates literally as the 'theatre of the capital'. The name originated with China's capital, Beijing, once regularly romanized as 'Peking' in the postal spelling. In most cases this book adopts the pinyin system of romanization, which is used in the People's Republic of China and is now the standard internationally. There are exceptions, however, and the primary one in this work is reference to Peking, not Beijing, Opera. 'Peking Opera' is still the accepted name, a familiar term in the English language and used widely in English-language publications in China and abroad.

While most of the illustrations included here are the author's own photographs, a number of individuals and organizations granted permission or supplied illustrations for this work. The photographs for Plates 1, 2, and 3 and Figures 1.1, 1.2, 1.3, 1.4, and 1.6 were taken, with permission, at the Exhibition on the History of Chinese Drama, arranged by the Traditional Drama Research Institute of the Chinese Arts Research Institute and housed at the headquarters of the Association of Chinese Dramatists in Beijing. The photograph for Figure 1.7 was taken, with permission, at the Tianjin Theatre Museum. Plate 6 is reproduced, with permission, from a slide purchased at the Mei Lanfang Memorial Museum. The photographs for Plates 18, 20, 21, and 22 were taken, with permission, at the Beijing Municipal Traditional Drama School. The photograph reproduced as Figure 2.8 is by Doug Smith. The photographs reproduced as Figures 1.5, 1.8, and 3.2 are by Hedda Morrison. Grateful appreciation is offered to all these contributors.

1

The History

In 1790 the Qianlong emperor (r. 1736–95), who presided over the greatest age of late imperial China, held massive celebrations in his capital, Beijing, to mark his eightieth birthday. Among the events honouring the occasion was the entry into the city of the Sanqing (Three celebrations) drama troupe from the southern province of Anhui.

One of the features of the Sanqing troupe was that the music of the items it performed combined two melodies. These were Erhuang, named after its place of origin, Yihuang, in Jiangxi province, and Xipi (literally, 'western skin' or 'western singing'), so called because it came from the western part of China. Although this musical combination had been popular in the southern provinces for several decades, it had not been heard in Beijing before Qianlong's celebration. Since its music still rests to this day on this same combination, it is legitimate to regard 1790 as the birth year of the Peking Opera.

Chinese Drama Before the Peking Opera

Long before 1790 there was a well-established dramatic tradition in China. In the south, performances with stories, impersonation, and relationships among the characters complex enough to qualify the items as 'drama' date from the early twelfth century, the style being called simply *nanxi* (southern drama). In the thirteenth century, the whole country, and especially the capital Beijing, underwent a golden age of drama which has provided themes for the theatre up to the present time. Although the thirteenth-century music has died out, and we know tantilizingly little about the costumes, gestures, and stagecraft of the time, a substantial body of scripts survives to this day. Most Chinese observers regard these scripts as their country's greatest corpus of drama from the point of view of literary merit.

The Ming (1368–1644) and early Qing (1644–1911) dynasties witnessed the growth and development of regional theatre in China. Each region had its own theatrical style based on local folk-songs, music, and dialect speech but generally with stories similar or identical from place to place. Most of these regional drama styles were popular theatre, meaning that their audiences were drawn from the common people (Plate 1).

There was, however, one drama style favoured by the educated élites and the aristocracy, including the imperial family and some of the emperors themselves, even the great

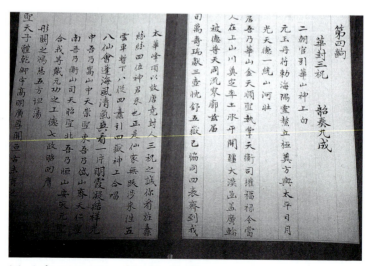

1.1 A drama script used by the Qianlong emperor.

Qianlong (Figure 1.1). This was Kunqu, meaning the 'tunes of Kun', so named because the place where it was developed into a coherent dramatic form was Kunshan, in Jiangsu province, very near today's Shanghai. The main characteristics of Kunqu were its elegant music and language, its slow regular rhythm, and accompaniment by the wistful sounds of the *dizi*, the Chinese side-blown flute. Kunqu produced a very fine and large literature of plays and many playwrights. The most famous of the dramatists was Tang Xianzu (1550–1617), who is sometimes called 'China's Shakespeare' in recognition of his fine reputation and because he was more or less a contemporary of the great English bard.

The educated men who wrote virtually all the surviving books of the time respected Kunqu but looked down on the popular theatre and its practitioners. It was just not done for them to attend a performance of popular theatre except as a censor, making sure that nothing subversive or improper occurred: texts of the time make frequent mention of 'men and women mixing unrestrainedly'. It follows that the surviving sources are biased against the popular theatre and might remain totally silent even about major developments within the genre.

Nevertheless, we know that the eighteenth century witnessed the growth of significant popular theatre traditions in several Chinese provinces, most notably Sichuan in the far south-west. One of the greatest actors in Chinese theatre history was the Sichuanese Wei Changsheng (1744–1802), who would probably have remained more or less unknown but for the fact that he brought a troupe to Beijing in 1779, became a star overnight, and saw the city serve not only as the country's political capital but, for the first time since the thirteenth century, its theatrical centre as well.

Wei was a female impersonator, and his art was distinctly risqué. This quality may have endeared him to the masses, but it irritated the authorities, who banned his art from the stage in 1785. A love affair with the famous but scurrilous Manchu politician Heshen (1750–99) saved him for a time, but he was forced to leave Beijing quite soon anyway. His main follower, Chen Yinguan, also favoured by several wealthy men as a lover as well as an actor, quit the city not long after Wei and for similar reasons. Despite provoking the authorities, Wei and Chen had made their mark on Beijing, and thereafter its audiences would not accept any but exciting theatre. It was in this context that the Sanqing troupe came to contribute to honouring Qianlong's birthday.

In artistic terms, one of Wei Changsheng's contributions was the development of *caiqiao*, stilted shoes which made it possible for actors to imitate the gait of a woman with bound feet (Figure 1.2). The shoes were so small that they could fit no more than the toes of a man's foot. The

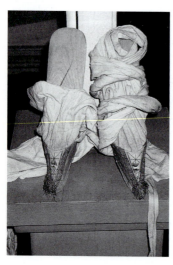

1.2 A pair of *caiqiao*. They would be tied to the feet with the cloth strips.

higher part of the shoe was tied around the lower part of the foot, with the actor in effect standing on tiptoe. Demonstration of this skill lasted until the 1950s, when the Communists suppressed it as unhealthy.

The Rise of the Peking Opera Before 1900

The Sanqing troupe was only the first of several companies from Anhui to come to Beijing. By the early nineteenth century four stood out from the rest and were dubbed the 'four great Anhui companies' (si da Huiban). In addition to the Sanqing troupe, these were the Chuntai (Spring stage), Hechun (Harmonious spring), and Sixi (Four joys) companies. These four drama troupes dominated the nineteenth-century Peking Opera, the Chuntai and Sixi companies surviving until the year 1900. Only in that year, in the midst of the Boxer Rebellion, did the burning of their theatres force the troupes to disband.

In the early years of the nineteenth century, the most prominent actors in Beijing were boys or young men who impersonated women. Through a kind of slave trade, entrepreneurs bought the boys in the south, primarily in Jiangsu and Anhui provinces, and took them to Beijing along the Grand Canal. Although the boys' parents signed contracts with the entrepreneurs which stipulated not only a price but when the boys would be returned to their homes, in fact there was absolutely nothing these poor people could do once their children had left for Beijing. Recruitment into the acting profession through purchase was nothing new in the nineteenth century, and it expanded greatly during those years as a result of deteriorating economic conditions throughout the country. It was a cruel system, to be sure, but it did provide a large pool of acting talent for the emerging Peking Opera. It was most certainly a major factor facilitating the quick growth of the Peking Opera during the last hundred years of the Qing dynasty.

Both on the way to Beijing and when they had reached the city itself, the boys began training in the difficult skills of the Peking Opera. Training schools were attached to all the main companies, the established actors taking on the new boys as disciples. Corporal punishment was common, with savage thrashings even for minor offences. It would be accurate, although incomplete, to say that the art of the Peking Opera was literally beaten into these boys.

Apart from practising their art as actors, the boys were frequently lovers to educated men. We know this to be the case from a range of poems which their admirers composed in their honour using the style of love poems to courtesans. Most admirers wrote under pen-names because of the social condemnation which homosexuals suffered. As it happened, female prostitutes were strictly outlawed in nineteenth-century Beijing, and it is possible that these boys filled at least a part of the gap created by their absence.

One of the more readily apparent differences between Western and Chinese dramatic forms is in categorization. The most important of all divisions in Western drama is generally seen as the distinction between tragedy and comedy. Although tragedy exists in Chinese theatre and comedy is enormously important to it, the focal division within it is between civil (wen) and military (wu) theatre. In Chinese civil theatre, the most common themes concern love, marriage, and relations between the sexes, and the central characters are usually women. In military theatre, on the other hand, the themes are war and power, the main characters are usually—although by no means always—men, and the climax is a spectacular display of acrobatics which represents battle.

It comes as no surprise that in the heyday of the boy actors early in the nineteeth century, most performances on the stages of Beijing were civil theatre, with the boys playing the roles of women. As the nineteenth century advanced, the more mature actors playing the roles of prime ministers, generals, and military men increasingly asserted themselves. The supply of boy actors from the south was cut off by the Taiping Rebellion, which wracked China, and especially its southern provinces, from 1851 to 1864. Boy recruits could still readily be found in the capital itself, and the second half of the nineteenth century is not short of fine female impersonators. Yet the emphasis of the Peking Opera as a whole clearly changed in these years to favour plays with military themes.

The nineteenth century saw several particularly outstanding *laosheng* (old male) actors, the performers of the distinguished male roles. Of these by far the most important was Cheng Changgeng (1811–80), a man whose contribution to the art was so great that he is sometimes called the 'father of Peking Opera'. This title recognizes that Cheng was the one person primarily responsible for integrating the different components he found into the complex whole we know today as Peking Opera. It was he who developed the various skills into a unified art, and who brought the status of Peking Opera to a new height. Indeed, many people regard the second half of the nineteenth century as the high point of the Peking Opera.

Cheng Changgeng modelled himself on the Confucian ideal: stern and upright, patriotic and hard-working, disciplined but expecting obedience from inferiors. Not only did he provide artistic leadership to the Sanqing troupe over several crucially important decades, thus contributing centrally to the artistic development of Peking Opera as a whole, but he was also very active in the actors' guild and was its most distinguished leader in the nineteenth century. In this capacity, he helped to raise the low social status of the acting profession. It remained low, of course, but Cheng's efforts had not been entirely in vain.

Another famous *laosheng* of the nineteenth century was Yu Sansheng (1802–66)(Plate 2). Whereas Cheng Changgeng was born in Anhui, Yu Sansheng came from Hubei province. Different forms of Erhuang and Xipi prevailed in the two provinces, and there were differences in the dialects of the libretti which underpinned the music. Under the influence of Cheng and Yu, Peking Opera was able to absorb both strains and unite them into an integrated whole.

The second half of the nineteenth century saw some of the Peking Opera's finest practitioners of both male and female character types (Plate 3). Outstanding among the famous *dan* (actors in female roles) were Shi Xiaofu (1846–1900) and Yu Ziyun (1855–99), the son of Yu Sansheng. Xu Xiaoxiang (1832–c.1882) was the best known of the *xiaosheng* (young male) actors, while among the *chou* (clown) characters, Yang Mingyu (Figure 1.3), born in 1815, was pre-eminent. (See Chapter 3 for a more detailed discussion of the role types.)

These men also established several acting families, their descendants continuing to shine for generations. Up to now, the longest lasting of these dynasties has been the six-generation Tan family. The famous *laosheng* Tan Xinpei (1847–1917) was the son of Tan Zhidao, a member of the Sanqing troupe, while his son Tan Xiaopei, grandson Tan Fuying, great-grandson Tan Yuanshou, and great-great-grandson Tan Xiaozeng all achieved prominence on the stage. The grandson of the *dan* Mei Qiaoling (1842–82) was Mei Lanfang (1894–1961), the most famous actor China has yet produced, and Mei Lanfang's son and daughter can still be seen in Peking Opera performances.

1.3 An original shirt used by the famous clown actor Yang Mingyu.

Another development of enormous importance in the history of the Peking Opera in the nineteenth century was its acceptance by the imperial court. As early as the eighteenth century the court had set up a special training school for actors, but it prepared them only for performance of the aristocratic and elegant Kunqu and certainly not the popular theatre. Moreover, virtually all those eligible to perform for the imperial family were eunuchs of the court or famous actors from the south.

In 1860 the court decided on a novel idea: to invite Peking Opera actors from the city to perform. The first performance celebrated the birthday of the Xianfeng emperor (r. 1851–61), but the experiment proved short-lived. Shortly after the imperial birthday, British and French troops occupied Beijing and the court fled to its summer residence at Jehol (now Chengde) to the north-east of the capital. By the time the crisis was over, Xianfeng was dead and the conservative forces who regarded it as an abomination to perform at court a popular form like Peking Opera again held sway.

In 1884 the Empress Dowager Cixi (1835–1908) revived the idea of having Peking Opera performed at court by actors from the city of Beijing. An avid enthusiast of the opera, she saw to it that this time the experiment would last. In the new Summer Palace, called Yiheyuan, she had two large stages built, so that she and her special invitees could watch performances in comfort and style (Plates 4 and 5). Within the imperial palaces themselves, she had a small stage erected in her own private quarters. The performers most often seen included some of the most popular of the day, among whom the most famous, and the Empress Dowager's favourite, was Tan Xinpei. Since no one from outside, let alone an actor, could enter the court without permission, these actors from the city needed a pass to enter the grounds. One dated 1908 and used by the

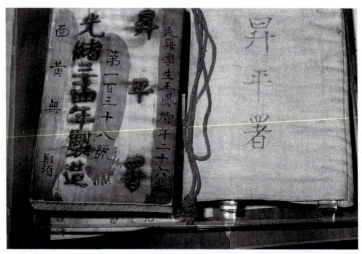

1.4 The work pass, dated 1908, which the actor Wang Fengqing used for permission to enter the palace.

1.5 A Chinese theatre in the 1930s, hats, teacups, and teapots arrayed along the edge of the stage. Photograph by Hedda Morrison.

laosheng actor Wang Fengqing (1883–1950) is still preserved in a Beijing museum (Figure 1.4). The characters on its front read *Shengping shu* (Rising peace office), the title of the government agency which managed the imperial actors.

As was the case in London and many other great cities of the time, a particular section of nineteenth-century Beijing, that located south of the Qianmen (Front gate), served as the city's theatre district. A substantial edifice, the Qianmen still stands proudly in the centre of Beijing on the southern extremity of massive Tiananmen Square. In the nineteenth century it marked the southern extremity of the Imperial City, accessible to commoners only on pain of death. In the theatre district, the most important concentration of theatres was in the narrow street called Dashala, which heads west from the main road leading south from the Qianmen.

The main theatres were also tea houses (Figure 1.5). There were gradations in standard according to the cost of where one sat, the better-off patrons sitting around tables with

1.6 A nineteenth-century *xigui*, on which was written the names of the plays to be performed each day.

food and tea provided. Prearranged plans dictated which troupes would perform on which days in which theatres, according to a rotation system. Troupes kept a special board, termed a *xigui* (Figure 1.6), which enabled the actors to find out what plays were to be performed that day. The *xigui* would be placed in the green room and a specially designated man, whose business was to find out the day's programme, would write the names of the items in and rub them out when finished, to make way for new ones.

The Boxer uprising of 1900 marked a major turning-point in the history of the Peking Opera. With the eight-power intervention in China to suppress the ragged peasants who had swarmed into the city from Shandong province, the great theatres of Beijing were all burnt down. This catastrophe led to the end of the system of nineteenth-century Beijing which had sustained the growth of the Peking Opera to maturity.

Tradition and the Challenge of Modernity, 1900 to 1949

Some aspects of the old Peking Opera system survived the Boxer catastrophe. One of these was the presence of Peking Opera at the imperial court. The court may have been forced to flee Beijing during the crisis, but on its return Tan Xinpei and others continued to visit it for the entertainment of the Empress Dowager.

Although Peking Opera survived the violence, the Boxer disaster brought to it great changes. In place of established troupes such as the four great Anhui companies, individual masters, Tan Xinpei among them, founded their own troupes. Several actors began to experiment with new content and new styles of the opera, for instance adopting themes

13

1.7 The 'four great famous *dan*' in the 1920s in their everyday clothes. In the front is Cheng Yanqiu; from right to left in the rear are Shang Xiaoyun, Mei Lanfang, and Xun Huisheng.

advocating social change. In Shanghai, centre of a prominent style of opera, Tan's son-in-law Xia Yuerun (1878–1931) was among a number of advocates of reform in the Peking Opera, as well as an active supporter of Sun Yatsen's revolution, which succeeded in overthrowing the Qing dynasty at the end of 1911. Western-style spoken drama, which was introduced from the West through Japan in the first decade of the twentieth century and promoted reformist and even revolutionary content, also exerted some influence on progressive Peking Opera actors.

Several famous actors dominated the Chinese stage in the first half of the twentieth century. Pre-eminent among them were Mei Lanfang and the three others in the quartet known as the 'four great famous *dan*' (*si da ming-dan*)(Figure 1.7). The quartet included Mei, Cheng Yanqiu (1904–58), Shang Xiaoyun (1900–76), and Xun Huisheng

(1900–68). Other particularly important actors in Beijing (renamed Beiping from 1928 to 1949) included the *laosheng* Yu Shuyan (1890–1943) and the *wusheng* (military male role) actor Yang Xiaolou (1877–1938), and, in Shanghai, the *laosheng* Zhou Xinfang (1895–1975).

Mei Lanfang (Plate 6) was the first of China's great actors to perform in the West, visiting the United States in 1930 and Europe in 1935. He was rapturously received on both occasions. In the United States, at the time suffering through the Great Depression, Mei played to full and enthusiastic houses. He drew ecstatic reviews, and the *New York World* declared him among the most extraordinary actors ever seen in that great and cosmopolitan city. In Europe, Mei met and performed in front of the German dramatist Bertolt Brecht (1898–1956) and exercised a tremendous influence over the European playwright. Indeed, not only did Brecht develop a lifelong enthusiasm for Chinese drama from seeing Mei's performances, but his influential theory of alienation arose from these experiences. This theory of acting argued that performers should not identify with the characters they were portraying, but rather should stand outside such characters, with the aim of producing a state of critical detachment, or alienation, from the play being presented. In Brecht's view, Chinese opera acting in general and Mei Lanfang's acting in particular contained brilliant exemplifications of this idea.

As a Chinese cultural ambassador to the West, Mei Lanfang has no rivals, but he was also important for his social contributions within China. His work undoubtedly helped raise the social status of Chinese actors, and he also helped to advance the prominence of female performers. By taking on the actress Xue Yanqin (1906–86) as a student in the 1930s, Mei took a courageous step in the atmosphere of the time. His decision showed that he was

1.8 Young actors in a Beijing garden in the 1930s. Photograph by Hedda Morrison.

prepared to risk public criticism by stepping out of line with social conventions. Xue went on to become the first great actress of traditional Chinese theatre in modern times, and was a pioneer by virtue of her regular appearances in mixed casts.

A new system of recruitment and training came into operation with the opening in 1904 of a special school for Peking Opera actors called the Xiliancheng (in 1912 renamed the Fuliancheng), to replace the training classes attached to the troupes. The new system was hard and enormous demands were made on the boys, who entered the school very young (Figure 1.8). But the school's system was far better than the one it replaced and served the Peking Opera well in the first half of the twentieth century. Mei Lanfang is one among several well-known actors of the Republican period trained in its halls. The school came on hard times in the late 1930s, especially during the Japanese occupation, and closed in 1948.

In 1930 the *Zhonghua xiqu zhuanke xuexiao* (China traditional drama school) was established. Although surviving for only eleven years and not achieving the same general success as did its predecessor, it was an advance on the Fuliancheng in several regards. Girls, as well as boys, were accepted as students. The curriculum included standard education in addition to the arts of the traditional theatre. Finally, although the emphasis remained on the Peking Opera, students could train also for the spoken drama.

Another school for drama in the late Republican period was the drama department of the Lu Xun Arts Academy, which the Chinese Communist Party (CCP) set up in Yan'an, in northern Shaanxi province, in October 1938. Yan'an was the headquarters of the CCP from the end of 1936 until 1947. Prior to establishing the academy, the Party had already developed a policy on the Peking Opera. In essence, the Party's tactic was to preserve the tradition but to reform it by making the masses the heroes in preference to those dubbed members of 'the feudal ruling classes'. Dramas about rebellions against the emperors and officials of old were praised, while those which presented 'feudal morality' in a good light were criticized. The CCP encouraged its authors and composers to create what were termed *xinbian lishi ju* (newly written historical dramas) which used traditional material but adapted it for revolutionary ends.

Peking Opera in the People's Republic

On 1 October 1949, following the victory of the Chinese Communist Party, Mao Zedong declared the founding of the People's Republic of China (PRC). Immediately, in theatre and in the other arts, the Party set about introducing the basics of its Yan'an policy more generally throughout the country. It set up schools to revive and encourage the Peking Opera, making sure that the students included both boys and girls and that they learned not only the skills of the theatre but a more general curriculum as well. It gave full encouragement to those actors who were prepared to support its policies and did what it could to raise their social status. It revived the traditional opera, but it also introduced reforms to it, censoring the content of the traditional operas to conform to its ideological demands and abolishing 'unhealthy' remnants, such as the shoes which enabled actors to imitate the gait of women with bound feet.

In 1958, Mao Zedong launched the Great Leap Forward in an unsuccessful attempt to push China's economic and social development forward with spectacular speed. At the time, the CCP introduced the slogan 'walking on two legs' in discussions both of the traditional theatre and of the economy. In the theatre, the 'two legs' were seen to be traditional and modern plays. On the whole, however, audiences did not react well to the modern themes, settings, and costumes, many regarding their introduction as a distortion of the opera. Performing traditional actions and gestures, and singing traditional music, to convey themes set in the present seemed ridiculous, while eliminating many of the traditional gestures and actions, and dressing the characters in contemporary costumes, seemed to take away the essence of Peking Opera itself.

18

In 1963, Jiang Qing, the wife of Mao Zedong and a former film actress, asserted herself in the world of Chinese political culture and especially in relation to the Peking Opera. She circulated a memorandum among senior leaders attacking 'ghost plays', that is, traditional operas, and demanding their removal from the stage. Naturally enough, this caused a storm of protest among traditionalists, who included many senior leaders such as Deng Xiaoping, at the time General Secretary of the CCP.

The following year, Jiang Qing and others organized a festival of Peking Opera on revolutionary and contemporary themes. Accompanied by a fanfare of propaganda, this festival heralded the almost total removal of traditional items from the stage. Worse was to follow. When Mao Zedong's Cultural Revolution erupted in 1966, attacks on the tradition became much more virulent. Not only were all performances of traditional opera banned, but records of their music and books about the operas were hunted from the market and destroyed.

One of the worst features of Jiang Qing's policies was the persecution of those artists she considered bourgeois or feudal. In regard to the Peking Opera, virtually every participant apart from a relatively few selected revolutionary performers suffered official condemnation. In particular, Jiang targeted nearly all of those who had excelled in the traditional opera, and many actors were humiliated, physically harmed, or otherwise persecuted by exuberant Red Guards fired up with revolutionary fervour.

The end of the Cultural Revolution came with the death of Mao Zedong on 9 September 1976 and, on 6 October, the fall of the Gang of Four, a quartet of ultraradical senior CCP leaders that included Jiang Qing. Early in November of that same year, attacks began on the role the Gang of

Four had played in the Chinese arts, including criticism of Jiang's theories of drama.

Deng Xiaoping, who had suffered demotion and persecution during the Cultural Revolution, was rehabilitated in mid-1977 and assumed supreme authority in China at the end of 1978. A long-time admirer of traditional theatre, Deng watched a series of performances in his home province of Sichuan during the Spring Festival of 1978, while on his way back from a trip to South-East Asia. The performers asked him directly if he would approve the revival of traditional dramas, and he answered with an enthusiastic yes. Almost immediately traditional theatre returned like a veritable flood throughout the country. A new heyday of traditional Peking Opera followed, while the troupes and audiences basked in their new-found freedom and exulted in their ability to see once again favourite plays they had not seen for ages, as well as creative, newly written works.

Unfortunately, this heyday was not to last. It was succeeded during the 1980s by a period of great uncertainty, with a major crisis caused by the disinterest of young people in the traditional arts, and especially in the Peking Opera. This last phase, and especially the situation in the 1990s, will be considered in the final chapter.

2

What Are Peking Operas About?

ASIDE FROM MYTHOLOGICAL ITEMS set in places such as the moon, virtually all Peking Opera takes place in territory that is now considered to be part of China. The great majority of pieces are set in a particular period of Chinese history and, in the old days, they were a rich source of knowledge about China's past. Indeed, it is not too much to say that local theatre styles, which include the Peking Opera, were a, or even *the*, major way that ordinary Chinese learned about the past of their own country. In this sense the dramas contributed enormously to feelings of a shared Chinese identity.

On the whole there is a great deal of reflection of historical fact in the plays. Many of the famous characters of Peking Opera did indeed exist at the times suggested in the dramas. There were in fact major civil wars among the three kingdoms of China in the third century of the Christian era. There were, as many of the plays suggest, efforts to resist encroachments from the north in the eleventh century. And Xuanzang, the Buddhist pilgrim in the Monkey King stories, did indeed go to India in search of Buddhist scriptures in the seventh century.

Of all the world's great cultures, China's is the most secular in its refusal to give political, educational, and even social power and influence to clerics, and the Peking Opera stories generally reflect this tradition. The majority of the stories, being based on historical fact, have no magic. However, it would be a great mistake to write off fantasy and myth. Some operas are set in the mythological period before any historical records. The Monkey King, defender of right and justice, may be the companion of the historical Xuanzang, but in fact he is a mythological character and his adventures show him fighting and winning against gods, demons, and spirits.

The Traditional Dramas

There are two main sources for the Peking Opera stories: older dramas and novels. Before the Peking Opera, there was a long tradition of drama which had found its way into the literary canon of China. The two most important of these groups of dramatic works are the northern pieces of the thirteenth and early fourteenth centuries and the southern Kunqu of the sixteenth to the eighteenth centuries. It is striking that the scripts of a very large number of these dramas have survived, even though the music of the northern dramas has long since died out. The Peking Opera as a genre derives from local operas, some of which themselves adapted the stories of these older plays. But some Peking operas come to us directly from Kunqu antecedents.

The other source of the stories is famous novels. Quite a few novels contribute to the canon, but as sources for the content of the Peking Opera four stand out as most important. These are *The Romance of the Three Kingdoms* (Sanguo yanyi), *Water Margin* (Shuihu zhuan), *Journey to the West* (Xiyou ji), and *The Romance of the Yang Family Generals* (Yangjia jiang yanyi).

The Romance of the Three Kingdoms deals with the civil wars of the third century AD. With the dissolution of the great Han empire in AD 220, three kingdoms established themselves: Shu in the south-west, Wu in the south-east, and Wei in the north. The wars among the three spawned stories of great heroism, of courage, treachery, loyalty, and patriotism. From ancient times these stories have been the stuff of storytellers and have entered the consciousness of the Chinese people.

2.1 A scene from *The Hu Family Village,* itself an episode from *Water Margin.* The rebels try to take the Hu village but are prevented by Hu Sanniang, in the military female role shown here.

Water Margin (Figure 2.1) is about a group of anti-government rebels based on Mount Liang, in Shandong province. The novel tends to present the rebels in a positive light, for which reason the Ming and Qing emperors issued many edicts against it. This condemnation did not prevent stories from the novel finding their way into the Peking Opera repertoire, although it must be remarked that they were far less numerous in the imperial period than in the years since the establishment of the republic in 1912.

Journey to the West concerns the monk Xuanzang's seventh-century visit to India in search of Buddhist sutras. Most important in the present context is that this novel includes the character of the Monkey King, who looms so

2.2 In *Havoc in Heaven,* the Monkey King is a general with four flags on his shoulders. He is shown here with members of his monkey army in his mountain forest lair.

large in Peking Opera for his struggle for right and against wrong. *Havoc in Heaven* (Nao Tiangong)(Figure 2.2) and *Havoc in the Dragon Palace* (Nao Longgong)(Figure 2.3), among the best-loved items in the repertoire, both show the Monkey King fighting and beating the forces of the gods.

The Romance of the Yang Family Generals tells the story of a family who resisted the invasion of the Liao people from the north in the early period of the Northern Song dynasty (AD 960–1127). Themes of patriotism and resistance to outside aggression are very powerful in the novel, as well as in the plays derived from it.

By far the most important way of categorizing the traditional Peking Opera is the division into civilian and military plays. Although each of these novels contains a great many military scenes, the fact that all but *Journey to the*

1. An illustration, taken from an edition of the novel *The Golden Lotus*, of a Ming dynasty performance in a private mansion of a style of regional southern drama. The orchestra is sitting in the front right.

2. The 'old male' actor Yu Sansheng.

3. Five of the thirteen famous late-Qing actors depicted by Shen Rongpu. From left to right they are the 'female role' Yu Ziyun, the 'old male' Cheng Changgeng, the 'young male' Xu Xiaoxiang, the 'female role' Shi Xiaofu, and the 'clown' Yang Mingyu.

4. The Great Stage inside the Deheyuan (Virtue and harmony garden) at the Summer Palace near Beijing, at which the Empress Dowager and her guests watched Peking Opera.

5. The Tingliyuan (Hall for listening to orioles), a stage at the Summer Palace, where the Empress Dowager watched Peking Opera from the comfort of a building opposite it.

6. Mei Lanfang in the role of Yang Yuhuan, favourite concubine of the eighth-century emperor Xuanzong, in the drama series *Unofficial History of the Imperial Concubine.*

7. In *Cao Cao and Yang Xiu*, because of his tyrannical nature the Chief Minister Cao Cao finds it impossible to trust anybody. The intellectual Yang Xiu, whom Cao eventually kills, is shown here in his grove.

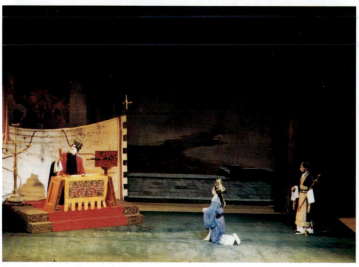

8. Cao Cao at his desk, in *Cao Cao and Yang Xiu*.

9. In *Heir Apparent Exchanged for a Leopard Cat*, the wicked concubine Liu confronts Kou Zhu (right), while her evil courtier looks on. Concubine Liu is trying to find out what Kou knows of a plot against her.

10. In this restored nineteenth-century painting of the Zhengyi Ci stage, all members of the audience are male and apparently well-to-do, one man having a substantial beard and looking to be a member of a Muslim minority.

11. A crossview of the Zhengyi Ci stage, as it appeared after being reopened late in 1995. One side of the stage itself is just visible on the right.

12. The stage of the Guangdong Guildhall in Tianjin features traditional, simple stage properties of a table and two chairs, and tables for tea and snacks for the audience.

13. On the pure traditional stage there are curtains at the back, but none in front. In this performance a stagehand pulls up the curtain for an actor to make his entrance.

14. In *Carrying a Wagon*, the *wusheng* Gao Chong (left) fights with a painted face enemy (right). Note the four flags on Gao's back and the spear and elaborate helmet of each character.

15. In the civilian drama *Three Claps of the Hand*, Wang Baochuan (centre), a *qingyi*, resists her father Wang Yun's orders concerning whom she should marry. An attendant stands on the left.

16. In more traditional Peking Opera, performances were introduced with items for good luck. The good-luck spirits wore masks, which are otherwise unusual in Peking Opera. This performance, showing the god of wealth, took place in the Zhengyi Ci stage, the characters above the actor meaning 'peace prevails throughout the world'.

17. Miming in the drama *The Crossroads*. Although the stage is lit normally, in the story the two characters are in total darkness. Neither knows the other is present, but each suspects there is another person in the room.

18. A cupboard holds spears and various military paraphernalia.

19. The People's Theatre in Beijing presents some of the country's best Peking Opera performances.

20. A ten-year-old 'painted face' actor and a male-role character practice miming the scene between Liu Lihua and Ren Tanghui in *The Crossroads*.

21. A seven-year-old *laodan* in training.

22. A student of female military roles goes through her paces under the guidance of a teacher.

2.3 In a scene from *Havoc in the Dragon Palace*, the Monkey King, pointing scornfully, fights off the soldiers of the Dragon King.

West are centred on military struggles does not mean that there are no civilian operas based upon them. Each play contains scenes with significant domestic family and love interest, including the treatment of issues of filial piety. Both *Water Margin* and *The Romance of the Yang Family Generals* have famous and still-performed items in which a hero's visit to his mother is at the core of the plot.

Both the Kunqu and the novels share one fundamental characteristic: they are episodic. Far too long for adaption to a short performance, they describe individual episodes but do not in themselves rise to a climax and denoument. Each of the episodes is easily adaptable for a short piece of about forty minutes in length. In some cases it is possible to put together episodes from the same novel for a more extended performance with some shared characters, but even then the drama will be episodic in nature, not climactic. Consequently, the dominant practice in the performance of Peking Opera since its beginning has been to present very short items one after the other in one session, rather than, as in the West, a longer single opera or play with consistent characters, a climax, and a denouement.

The division between comedy and tragedy, so crucial to Western drama, is much less important to the Peking Opera. In fact, there is no highly developed theory of comedy and tragedy in the Chinese literary tradition. The concept that the essence of tragedy resides in the unsuccessful struggle of the hero against his own fate is, not surprisingly, totally absent from the Chinese world. On the whole, the Chinese do not like a sad ending. The battle scenes generally show the good character and his or her men victorious, and although some of the enemy may be killed, this is not represented by actors dropping down on the stage but by rapid exiting.

On the other hand, there is plenty of humour, seriousness, and sadness in Chinese theatre. Indeed, small-scale, short items about matchmakers and happy outcomes in love are based on light-hearted comedy. There is even comedy in some of the battle scenes, for instance those in which the Monkey King plays a prominent role. Of course, seriousness is the dominant tone in the items that treat civil war or rebellion. Although it is rare, there are a few plays which end with the death or suicide of the hero. The famous *Farewell to My Concubine* (Bawang bieji) (Figure 2.4) ends with the suicide of the concubine and the immediate defeat and death of the general, Xiang Yu. The conclusion of *The Li Ling Stele* (Li Ling bei)(Figure 2.5) comes with the suicide of General Yang Jiye, who has been defeated and sees no way out of his troubles. In neither case is the death represented on stage. In *The Li Ling Stele*, Yang is said to dash himself against a stone stele dedicated to Li Ling, a defeated general of ancient times, but there

2.4 In *Farewell to My Concubine*, Xiang Yu, defeated by the Han emperor Liu Bang, bids farewell to his favourite concubine, who commits suicide after performing a ritual dance.

2.5 *The Li Ling Stele* tells the story of Yang Jiye, who is defeated in battle and commits suicide by dashing himself against the stele of Li Ling, a defeated general of the Han dynasty.

is no stele on the stage and the suicide is simply left to the audience's imagination.

The fight for justice, which comes through strongly in many works of the Peking Opera, shows that there is a moral side to the content of the plays. It is true that entertainment was of paramount importance in the performances, but there were values inherent in the dramas as well. Many promoted the standard tenets of Confucianism, with its emphasis on filial piety and the maintenance of a strong hierarchy within society. But there was enough of the rebel spirit in the stories of the Peking Opera, as well as other local styles of drama, that the government kept a sharp eye out for what was happening on the stage and issued numerous proscriptive edicts if it did not like what it found. The Qing court had stories about rebellion bowdlerized before it allowed them to be performed on its stages.

The Modern Period

Very few literary figures wrote for the Peking Opera until the early years of the twentieth century. One of the developments of the Republican period was the association of a few distinguished literary figures with famous actors. Such men wrote plays and acted as propagandists specifically for their performing friends, the pieces created being termed *xinxi* (new plays). In contrast with the purely traditional items, the *xinxi* had a coherent plot and occupied a full evening. By far the most important and well-known of the associations between writer and actor was that between Mei Lanfang and Qi Rushan (1877–1962). Qi wrote more than forty operas, as well as an enormous amount about the history and current circumstances of the Peking Opera.

In sponsoring the composition of *xinbian lishi ju* in Yan'an during the 1940s, the CCP dictated content which followed the Party's ideological prescriptions. In other respects these 'newly written historical dramas' had much in common with the *xinxi*. In formal terms, they still followed the traditional categorization of actors, and the music was in traditional style. But the plot was to rise to a climax, being thus different from the episodic structure of the traditional Peking Opera, and each play was designed to provide a full evening's entertainment.

In December 1943 an opera of the new style was premièred in Yan'an. Entitled *Driven up Mount Liang* (Bishang Liangshan), it was based on the novel *Water Margin* and showed its hero forced to join the rebellion by government oppression. In January 1944 Mao Zedong himself wrote a letter to the actors, praising them for seizing the stage from the traditional scholars and beauties and giving it to the people.

When the CCP came to power in 1949, it not only had many of the traditional items and *xinxi* censored and removed from the stage, but it also reformed the remainder to emphasize what Mao Zedong had called 'the democratic essence' of the imperial period. In the Party's view, dramas should be patriotic, give centre stage to representatives of the people but criticize those of the ruling classes, and pay proper respect to women and minorities. The CCP made sure that the *xinbian lishi ju* had appropriately proletarian themes.

A few items in Peking Opera form have been written with settings in the present or the very recent past. One such piece is *The White-Haired Girl* (Baimao nü), a drama with a strongly revolutionary theme which had been premièred as a modern opera in Yan'an in April 1945. It was not until the 1964 festival (see Chapter 1), however, that operas which focused on lauding the CCP and its heroes came to dominate the stage. *The Story of the Red Lantern* (Hongdeng ji), for example, set during the war against Japan, concerns the fate of three generations of revolutionaries. In the end, two of the three are executed by the Japanese, but the youngest helps the Communist guerrillas to score a major victory. In this as in other portrayals of the Revolution, all personal tragedies are balanced against the triumph of the cause.

When the Cultural Revolution broke out in 1966, Jiang Qing devised a theory of 'model' dramas, according to which she had the items that had been performed at the 1964 festival revised and restaged. The main principles of this theory were that the plays of the Peking Opera should reflect class struggle, promoting the interests of the proletariat, particularly members belonging to or associated with the Party, and denouncing bourgeois villains, who took the form of Guomindang officials, their representatives, or the Japanese occupiers. Western instruments were added to the orchestra to make the music sound more heroic and revolutionary. In practice, Jiang Qing's theories brought about the excercise of extreme censorhip, because virtually nothing could be performed which Jiang herself had not directly approved.

No sooner was Mao Zedong dead and the Gang of Four overthrown in the northern autumn of 1976 than Jiang Qing's theories were criticized. In 1977, *Driven up Mount Liang*, which had been disallowed performance during the Cultural Revolution despite Mao's praise for it in 1944, staged a comeback. The traditional dramas returned to the stage like a flood.

One of the most interesting features of the 1980s in the world of the Peking Opera was the large number of newly created historical dramas that were premièred during those years. Like their counterparts before the Cultural Revolution, these new pieces carried political implications. They still

30

tended to give play and a political role to women and minorities, and they were still patriotic, but they were much less concerned with issues of class. The peasant rebels on whom the CCP had earlier heaped such praise and to whom it had accorded centre stage tended to withdraw in favour of those people 'who had made a contribution to the Chinese nation'. Such people could readily include officials or members of the feudal ruling classes. Of course, emperors were sometimes negative characters but were not necessarily so.

Unfortunately, scriptwriters and composers appear to be producing far fewer newly written historical dramas in the 1990s than in the 1980s, and of the good material still coming forth virtually none is from Beijing. The rather small number of items on contemporary themes written in the 1980s has dwindled still further. The reasons for this decline are complex, but in the main China has become an extremely money-oriented society, and there is just very little to be gained from writing new pieces for the Peking Opera.

One strong trend in the 1980s and 1990s is the return of operas banned or out of favour in earlier times. For instance, the revolutionary dramas of the 1964 festival and Jiang Qing's models went out of favour with the death of Mao Zedong, but some are again performed and well-received in the late 1980s and 1990s. A performance of *The Story of the Red Lantern* in Beijing late in 1995 was sold out and the response of the audience to it was very positive.

Some Sample Dramas

There are numerous Peking operas. In 1980, the *Zhongguo xiju chubanshe* (Chinese theatre press) in Beijing published a Chinese-language compilation of Peking Opera stories edited by the specialist Tao Junqi. It contained no fewer than 1,220 items, which preliminary investigation had shown to be complete, although naturally items dating from the years since the work was finished are not included. Rather than attempting to be comprehensive, I have selected here just four sample operas, adding to the above comments and supplemented by the picture captions.

In addition to *The Li Ling Stele*, mentioned above for its sad ending, one of the most popular of the Yang family dramas is *Women Generals of the Yang Family* (Yangmen nüjiang). The drama is a *xinbian lishi ju* completed in 1960.

Women Generals of the Yang Family (Figure 2.6) opens with the dowager She Taijun celebrating her hundredth birthday. China is again threatened from the north and the court is thinking of compromise. Because the only male

2.6 In *Women Generals of the Yang Family*, She Taijun, second from left. the centenarian dowager of the Yang family, plans a successful attack to effect the release of Yang Wenguang, the youngest of the male fighters of the Yang family.

left in this family of generals is too young to take the lead in war, the dowager urges the women to go out and fight. This they do, especially Mu Guiying, the widow of one of the Yangs, and they defeat the enemy spectacularly.

The drama's political message is that women, along with men, should take part in politics and the defence of the country and, like most of the new historical dramas, it is appropriate to its age of composition. But Mu Guiying is one of quite a few female military leaders in the Peking Opera and is in no way a creation of the PRC. Confucianism did not give women any substantial role in politics or the army, and Chinese history is significantly lacking in female military heroes. Given this historical reality, the presence of female military heroes in the Peking Opera is quite remarkable.

Two dramas from Shanghai figured prominently at the First Festival of Peking Opera Arts (*Shoujie Jingju yishu jie*) held in Tianjin in November 1995 and were performed there by the Shanghai Peking Opera Company (*Shanghai Jingju yuan*). *Cao Cao and Yang Xiu* (Cao Cao yu Yang Xiu), which won first prize at the festival, dates from 1988, while *Heir Apparent Exchanged for a Leopard Cat* (Limao huan taizi), arranged from dramas originally created in the 1920s, was new, having been premièred in Shanghai earlier that month.

Cao Cao and Yang Xiu (Plate 7) is based on the novel *The Romance of the Three Kingdoms*, but it contains some creative modifications. Both the central characters of the title are actual historical figures, and the story takes place before the fall of the Han dynasty in AD 220. The plot concerns the tyrant Cao Cao, who enlists the services and advice of his son-in-law, the scholar Yang Xiu, a straightforward and honest man who is somewhat careless in what he says. At first the relationship is good, but Cao Cao is the kind of leader who cannot tolerate any opposition or questioning. He kills another of his devoted followers, Kong Wendai, suspecting his loyalty, and then regrets his hastiness. In the end, he has Yang Xiu executed for similar reasons (Plate 8).

The characterization of this drama is quite subtle and complicated, entirely unlike traditional Peking Opera. Cao Cao is portrayed as paranoid—this writer was reminded very forcefully of Mao Zedong—but not without redeeming features. The underlying theme of the tension between political masters, represented by Cao Cao, and intellectuals, exemplified by Yang Xiu, is skilfully interwoven into the developing relationship between the two central characters. The plot rises to a climax and tragic denouement, having thus developed greatly from the generally episodic nature of traditional Peking Opera.

The plot of *Heir Apparent Exchanged for a Leopard Cat* concerns two concubines, surnamed Li and Liu, of the emperor Zhenzong (r. 998–1022) of the Northern Song dynasty. Emperor Zhenzong decrees that the first of the two to have a son will become empress, while the other will be put under house arrest in the 'cold palace'. Li's son is born first, but in a fit of rage and jealousy her rival Liu, whose character is strikingly similar to that of the latter-day Jiang Qing, conspires with her evil courtier Guo Huai to exchange the baby for a leopard cat and to convince the Emperor that the baby is a demon (Figure 2.7). Liu also conspires to have the baby thrown into the moat and tries to get her maid servant Kou Zhu to carry out the deed. Kou refuses, however, and with the help of the good minister Chen Lin saves the baby. Liu's own son dies, but she becomes empress nonetheless, while Li is imprisoned.

Seven years later the heir apparent, now a little boy, not knowing she is his mother, goes with Kou Zhu in atten-

2.7 In a scene from *Heir Apparent Exchanged for a Leopard Cat*, the good courtier Chen Lin, amid the elaborate and beautiful scenery of the imperial garden, is seen carrying the cradle where the baby heir apparent ought to be sleeping but which in fact contains a leopard cat.

dance to see Concubine Li where she remains in the cold palace (Plate 9). The Empress Liu finds out about the visit through Guo Huai and is furious. To find out the details of what transpired during the meeting, and to prevent a change of verdict by the Emperor over who should be empress, Empress Liu has Kou whipped savagely and orders Chen Lin to interrogate and beat her. Kou refuses to divulge any information about the meeting and dies under the blows. In the end of this section of the drama, Li's warder in the palace agrees to let her out and burns it down as Li escapes.

By way of balance to these grim stories, we might conclude with a highly comic one. Set in the Tang dynasty (AD 618–907), *Chuncao Storms the Court* (Chuncao chuang-tang) concerns the daughter of the prime minister and her marriage to a young man who first protects her from a molester but is then prosecuted for murdering him. How such material can become the stuff of comedy rests on the role of Chuncao, the daughter's maidservant, as the play's central character. The court sentences the young man to death, but Chuncao enters to tell the magistrate that he is the future son-in-law of the prime minister. When the magistrate goes to the prime minister's house to check the story with him (Figure 2.8), Chuncao persuades the daughter to confirm the match. In the end this comic make-believe becomes reality and the couple are happily married.

The play is based on a traditional story. It was reformed in the 1960s in very traditional style to occupy a full evening and is still performed in the 1990s. Comedy and righted

2.8 In *Chuncao Outwits the Magistrate*, the corrupt magistrate, a clown character, discusses matters with the prime minister, an 'old male', with other officials behind. Photograph by Doug Smith.

injustice have been the stuff of traditional Chinese drama since its beginnings and it is striking that they remain significant even today.

3

The Performance Arts

IT IS THE COMBINATION of performance arts used within it which makes the Peking Opera so distinctive and so fascinating. While there have been marvellous singers of the music, such as Mei Lanfang, to an extent far greater than with Western opera it is only when one has the opportunity to see Peking Opera on the stage that one can appreciate it properly. Of course we miss the spectacle if we merely listen to the music of a masterpiece like Giuseppe Verdi's *Aida* without seeing the costumes, sets, and performance styles, and there is pleasure to be gained by appreciating the great Chinese voices of the past. But the integration of all the arts matters much more to Peking Opera than to its Western counterparts.

The Stage

The old-style Chinese stage was square, with two poles on either side at the front and the audience seated on three sides. Several of these traditional stages survive in Beijing, especially in the Summer Palace and other previously aristocratic quarters, as well as one in Tianjin.

One stage of particular interest lies outside the Heping Men (Peace gate) not far from what used to be the main theatre centre of Beijing. Called the Zhengyi Ci (Zhengyi temple) stage (Plate 10), it was built in the middle of the seventeenth century in what was at that time a temple. The list of famous actors who performed on it is a long one, including Cheng Changgeng, Tan Xinpei, Mei Qiaoling, and Mei Lanfang. When the Japanese occupied Beijing in

1937, however, it fell into more or less total disuse. It was not until October 1995 that the stage was reopened for Peking Opera performances (Plate 11).

Another stage of interest is found in the Guangdong Guildhall in Tianjin (Plate 12). Unlike the Zhengyi Ci stage, it is no longer used for performances. Built in 1907, it was the site of a famous speech by the great nationalist leader Sun Yatsen, a native of Guangdong, in August 1912. Many famous Peking Opera actors, including Mei Lanfang, Xun Huisheng, Shang Xiaoyun, and Yang Xiaolou performed on the stage, as did many artists of other regional styles. In 1986 the building was converted into the Tianjin Theatre Museum (*Tianjin xiju bowuguan*).

In the purest form of traditional Peking Opera, the stage is almost completely bare, with a great deal left to the imagination. One sees a curtain at the back of the stage, but not the front, and a carpet on the floor. One never finds such a thing as a door on the traditional stage, following the principle that what is interesting about a door is not the door but what happens behind it. Stage properties are simple, usually no more than a table and a chair or two. In old-style performances, a special actor with no character role opens the curtain at the back of the stage for the actors to enter, generally from the left seen from the point of view of the audience, and moves the stage properties as necessary (Plate 13).

In the modern theatres, it is now customary to draw the curtains to show the beginning and end of the scene, even for the most traditional pieces. This practice follows the common pattern in Western opera. In presentations of the *xinbian lishi ju*, the modern historical dramas, and of those plays on contemporary themes, the decoration of the stage has changed drastically. There is often complex and realistic scenery at the back of the stage, with not much left to the imagination. At times there is also quite complicated scenery, such as a city wall or a room with a door, at the centre of the stage. In other words, the newly composed Peking operas show heavy Soviet and Western influence in abandoning the traditional simplicity of stage presentation.

Role Types

In Western opera the categorization of roles generally follows the distinctions of vocal range, with gender implied in those distinctions: soprano, mezzo-soprano, tenor, baritone, and bass. In the Peking Opera categories, and indeed those of other forms of Chinese drama, vocal range is not a central factor, but the gender of the character is essential, with age, social status, rank, and personality being important as well. Another factor which enters into the role types is the division so crucial to all Chinese drama, that between civilian and military.

In the *nanxi* of the twelfth and later centuries there were seven role types, and they form the basis for later styles of Chinese theatre, the Peking Opera included. Among the seven were the *sheng* ('male roles'), *dan* ('female roles'), *jing* ('painted face'), *chou* ('clown'), and *mo* ('supporting male role'). In this group only the *dan* was a female role, the others being male. The *sheng* meant simply the main male character, while the *mo* was a supporting male role, who also fulfilled the function of beginning the drama by revealing the plot to the audience. The *jing* was the 'painted face', while the *chou* was the clown, whose face was ugly and daubed with black powder.

It is not necessary for our discussion to trace how these various role types developed over the centuries. They remain central to the Peking Opera, however, for an understanding of whose style their treatment requires more detail. In the Peking Opera of the mid-nineteenth century there were ten basic role types, which was reduced to seven in the first half of the twentieth century. After 1949, the number was further reduced, firstly to five and very soon after to four, namely *sheng* (male roles), *dan* (female roles), *jing* or *hualian* ('painted faces' roles), and *chou* (clowns). These four carry the same basic meaning as in the ancient southern drama of the twelfth century. However, there are also some interesting subcategories in these four role types.

Among the five subgroups of *sheng* and numerous sub-subgroups, three stand out as the most important and striking (Plate 14). These are the *laosheng* ('old male roles'), the *wusheng* ('military male roles'), and *xiaosheng* ('young male roles'). The *laosheng* are the educated and dignified men, the officials, and emperors. Generally the *laosheng* are high in social status, or have been so, and wear beards. The *xiaosheng* are the scholar–lovers, the younger men of letters. They sing falsetto and never wear beards. The *wusheng* are the generals or any male characters who take part in battles. It is possible to combine the last with either of the other two, as in, for instance, the *wuxiaosheng* ('military young male role')(Figure 3.1), the young general or fighter skilled in the martial arts.

Peking Opera's female roles can be subdivided in ways similar to those that distinguish between the males. The main subcategories of female roles are the *qingyi* (a young lady), *huadan* ('flower female role'), the *wudan* ('military female role'), and the *laodan* ('old female role'). The *qingyi* is the filial daughter, devoted wife or lover, and the good mother (Plate 15). She is generally demure in character and subdued in action, tending to look downwards. The *huadan* is more vivacious and flirtatious, and sometimes even of

41

3.1 At the Beijing Municipal Traditional Drama School, a student of the military male roles, with the standard four flags and spear, is coached in the correct movements by his teacher.

questionable character. The *wudan* is the female fighter, skilled in the military arts. The *laodan* is the old mother or other aged woman.

Until the 1930s there were hardly any mixed-gender troupes in the Peking Opera, with female roles almost always played by men. The female impersonator has been a major characteristic of the traditional Peking Opera, and indeed virtually all other local styles of drama in China since the Ming dynasty. In the 1930s, however, a few actresses began to take part in Peking Opera in female roles. When the Communists came to power, they laid down the principle that men should play male roles and women female ones. The female impersonator Zhang Junqiu, who was born in 1920 in Jiangsu province, related to me in 1980 that Zhou Enlai, the Prime Minister of China from 1949 until his death in January 1976, had said to him, 'Up to you the male *dan* and that's the end'. In the early 1980s I met a young trainee male *dan* in Nanjing, but in the mid-1990s he is virtually the only young professional male *dan* in China. The number of older ones is vanishingly small, one of these very few being Mei Lanfang's son, Mei Baojiu. It is apparent that the old art of the male *dan* will soon die out, with women performing all except comic female roles.

The 'painted face' characters are usually statesmen, warriors, heroes, demons, or swashbucklers. They can be divided into civilian (*wenjing*) or military (*wujing*) roles, with the latter generally highly skilled in martial arts. Their personality is shown by the patterns and colours of the paint on their faces, a topic to be discussed in more detail below.

The clowns wear a patch of make-up around their nose and eyes; this patch is now white, not black as in the twelfth century. The clowns are often funny, foolish, or awkward men, mostly positive characters, simple and sincere, but occasionally villains or traitors. Except in a comedy, a clown is never the lead character. Like the other role types, a clown can be either civilian or military, with the latter being expert in acrobatics.

In the Peking operas on contemporary themes, especially Jiang Qing's model operas, the role categories tend to break down. Although of course there were—and are—still male and female roles, the painted face disappears completely and the faces of the clown characters no longer have white patches. The *xinbian lishi ju* retain the traditional role categorizations but also use other methods, such as the libretti and the music, to convey the personalities clearly, and so the categories are not nearly as important from a theatrical point of view as in the past.

Costumes and Headgear

Peking Opera compensates for the simplicity of the stage and props with very complex, and usually highly colourful and splendid, costumes and headgear. As with so much else in the Peking Opera, each costume is designed to fit the gender, personality, calling, and status of the character. Other mismatching features are of little importance: all costumes are based on the clothing of the Ming dynasty, no matter in which period the play is set, and characters wear the same costumes no matter the season in which the story takes place.

One reason why the costumes are so magnificent is because of the prevalence of robes, especially ceremonial ones. Use of ceremonial robes was originally reserved for members of the royal family and the aristocracy, but the eighteenth-century emperor Qianlong, having seen them in use in a local Kunqu performance, ordered their use in drama. After a period the costumes of the Peking Opera became more and more elaborate, until in the 1930s the Shanghai actor Zhou Xinfang felt it necessary to simplify and reform the men's robes.

Zhou's contribution notwithstanding, the robes of the Peking Opera remain one of its most colourful and grandest features. The most magnificent of the ceremonial robes are those worn by an emperor, which are yellow with a large coiled dragon symbolizing imperial power. Ceremonial robes used as costumes include a circular belt, termed a 'jade belt' (*yudai*) in Chinese, always too large a circle to hold any clothes in place but symbolic of authority and adding to the splendour of the dress. Emperors also wear decorated crowns with tassles hanging down.

Armour came into vogue in Peking Opera in the 1860s, with the growth in significance of the military plays at that time. Like the robes, the armour of generals or other senior officers in military plays is very elaborate and colourful, whether worn by male or female characters. Many generals, male and female alike, have four flags attached to their back to increase the impression of power and valour. There is also an astonishing variety in the shape, colour, and design of helmets, which add to the variety and fascination of the costuming.

Though less elaborate than the robes or armour, the coats worn by a variety of characters ranging from literati to young ladies or poor women also illustrates the complexity of Peking Opera costumes. Although these come in many colours, the bluish coats of poor women are of special interest, in that the term 'bluish clothes' (*qingyi*) has come to be used for the demure, although not necessarily poor, female characters. For some female roles the 'flowing sleeve' (*shuixiu*) attached to the coat is highly significant. A feature of dancers' costumes from ancient times in China, this overlong sleeve is attached to the coats of actors in some female roles. In the hands of a skilled actor, it is possible to inject great artistry into shaking down the flowing sleeve to fit the length of the arm and show the hand. A particular master in the arts of the flowing sleeve was one of the 'four great famous *dan*', Cheng Yanqiu, who designed several gestures to manipulate it more gracefully.

The costumes have become one of the defining features of the traditional items based on old stories. The term *guzhuang xi*, which means literally 'ancient costume drama', has come to refer to any items that treat traditional themes. In the Peking operas on contemporary themes, the costumes and headgear are very much more realistic and simple than in the traditional pieces. In these, the appearance and colour of the dress clearly show not only the

45

character's role but the period, season, and context of the scene itself.

Adorning the Face

Make-up is used for all categories of actors in Peking Opera. On the whole, however, it is very much more simple for the *sheng* and *dan* than for the 'painted face' roles or the clowns. Comparing the 'painted face' roles and the clowns, make-up is much more important to the former than to the latter.

The overall purpose of make-up to the Peking Opera is to make the actor's face look like that of the character he or she is trying to portray, both in reality but—more important—symbolically. This intention generally results in quite a bit of exaggeration of characteristics, since, where the two conflict, artistry takes precedence over realism. If the actor's eyes are too small for the character, for example, he may enlarge them by blackening his eye sockets.

For *sheng* and *dan* roles, it is generally enough to apply powder and rouge to the face, and not to paint it. The lips and the area around the eyes must be reddened, especially for the female roles. Apart from those playing *xiaosheng*, actors in most male roles wear beards, sometimes wispy, sometimes thick and luxuriant, and sometimes very long, but with different styles characteristic of the person the actor is playing. These beards almost always cover the mouth. They are attached around the upper lip, not to the cheek and chin, and flow downwards. They are in no sense meant to represent moustaches.

The painted face is one of the most distinctive features of the Peking Opera. Although it is not the only form of Chinese theatre in which some characters have a painted face, this art is far more highly developed in Peking Opera than in any other style of Chinese drama.

The painted face developed over the centuries from masks. Used in ceremonial dances in ancient times, masks have survived in certain forms of local opera, especially a whole group of folk drama styles termed *nuo*, which are found in southern China, especially Guizhou province. In Tibetan drama the mask is still very common, with some showing animal heads and others symbolizing features of personality. In the Peking Opera the mask is very rare nowadays. It does survive for a very limited number of characters, however, such as the god of wealth who appears in the introductory good luck items in highly traditional performances (Plate 16).

The painted face is not merely beautiful and complex; it is a highly symbolic art. There are two main features of the make-up: colour and design. The combination enables the audience to identify the character immediately and to discern something about his or her personality. Is he or she a character with whom one should sympathize, a villain, or someone in between these two? The actor accentuates the symbolism of the painted face by exaggerating the feature he is trying to show, be it anger, good nature, integrity, or whatever.

A wide range of colours is used on the face, including red, purple, black, white, blue, green, and yellow. Although these colours were originally intended to enhance the natural complexion of the character, they gradually came to represent the temperament of the characters. It is rare for a painted face to have a single colour only. Most colours suggest good characteristics—red symbolizes courage and loyalty, purple bravery and wisdom, black seriousness and integrity—but some symbolize ugly features, such as watery white, which denotes treachery and cruelty, and yellow,

3.2 His face intricately painted and composed, an actor mimics the posture of the Monkey King. Photograph by Hedda Morrison.

which is associated with brutality. There are exceptions, of course, to these general principles, and some colouring still merely enhances natural complexion.

In addition to the actor's use of colour on the face, temperament, status, and mood are also shown by the design of pattern. Some characters are shown with angry or honest patterns on their face, to suggest the kind of person they are. The pattern might also be designed to resemble an animal. The most obvious and important example of this, seen in dramas based on the novel *Journey to the West*, is the Monkey King (Figure 3.2), whose narrow face and full eyes closely resemble those of a monkey. One of the Monkey King's enemies is the White Elephant, who is shown with a white face, a trunk, and two tusks.

Designing and applying the paint demands great care and artistry. Just as with painting, the brush strokes must be both accurate and forceful, in order to arrive at exactly the correct colour and design, thereby to give the right impression to the audience. Some actors develop their own techniques and designs to accord with how they see the role they are trying to play. It is in fact part of the skill of a painted-face actor to understand and master the process of painting itself.

Although the design of the painted face is most important to the *jing* roles, it has its place as well in the refinement of the clowns' appearance. The white patch over the nose and around the eyes is common to all the clowns, but the shape of the patch varies greatly. It may be elongated, covering only the nose and avoiding the cheeks altogether, or it may be square, triangular, or diamond-shaped but covering some of the cheeks and forehead. A skilful actor can produce comical effects through caricature in applying the white paint. Just as with the *jing* characters, clowns vary greatly in temperament, and the style of the white paint gives an indication of the sort of person the actor intends to portray.

Movements and Gestures

The movements and gestures of the Peking Opera are highly stylized. The way performers move, mime, walk, stand and sit, point their finger, and stroke their beard says as much about their abilities as performers as do their method of singing and their articulation of the words of the lyrics. Three aspects of movement and gesture deserve special treatment: mime, walking style, and acrobatics.

Mime is central to the action in some of the non-military plays. A young woman acts out threading a needle, sewing, and then breaking the thread at the end, or feeding chickens by scattering grain, even though in both cases she is in fact working in thin air. In an extended mime scene in *The Crossroads* (Sanchakou), a military item based on an ancient folk-tale, the characters Ren Tanghui and Liu Lihua move in such a way as to suggest that each cannot see the other, and is not even sure where the other is, although the stage is fully lit (Plate 17). Most of *Autumn River* (Qiu jiang), a civil play set in the Song dynasty (960–1279), takes place on a boat. Escaping from her convent, the young nun Chen Miaochang and the boatman who helps her first mime setting off from the shore and then register the impact of wind and wave, as part of punting across the river in autumn (Figure 3.3). Finely performed, the overall effect is perfect theatre.

Another feature of the movement of Peking Opera is walking, the style suiting the particular category of performer, whether a young male, a female, or another type. Men tend to strut, taking large and very deliberate steps. Other than as military figures, however, women walk much more gently and slowly. The *qingyi* characters walk by way of very quick but very short steps which, when performed properly, give the impression of grace and femininity. The *huadan* characters walk more quickly and deliberately, but still with very short steps. In the courtship scenes with *qingyi* and *xiaosheng* roles, the contrast between the cock-like male strides and the simpering, subordinate female gait is very striking.

50

3.3 In this scene from *Autumn River*, the boatman on the right mimes punting, while the nun mimes the instability of riding on a boat.

One of the most characteristic of all the features of Peking Opera is the acrobatics or gymnastics of the battle scenes. An evening of several short Peking Opera items almost always ends with such a display. The acrobatics usually consist of somersaulting, doing a series of cartwheels very quickly, and throwing spears, swords, and other paraphernalia around with lightning speed and perfect accuracy (Plate 18). A high point is the double spear toss in which a general, usually a woman, kicks two spears at once in opposite directions, one with each foot. The person at whom a spear toss is directed also has a big responsibility, for there is nothing more shameful than for a performer to miss the catch. The speed and precision of these acrobatic displays have to be seen to be believed, and they are certainly one of the main thrills of a Peking Opera performance.

3.4 Formerly, the orchestra at a Peking Opera performance would sit on the stage, but it is now most often located to the side.

Music and Musical Instruments

The importance of music to Peking Opera is evident from the common phrase *ting xi*, which is taken to mean 'going to the opera' but, more literally, means 'listening to theatre'. The paramount reason for going to the Peking Opera, it appears, is to listen to the music (Figure 3.4). To this day, many people hum along with the melodies as they watch the action on stage.

In the earlier drama styles of the south, such as Kunqu, dramatists chose from already existing tunes and wrote words to fit the tune selected. In the north, however, and in particular in Peking Opera, the system was reversed, similar to the pattern familiar in the West. The lyrics set the metre, with the music designed to fit their rhythmic requirements.

In Peking Opera, the music is tightly blended into the whole experience, with the different characters singing in very different styles. Consequently, the *qingyi* characters sing much more demurely and generally much more slowly than do the *jing*. Sometimes, particular characters sing special melodies different from those sung by others.

The basic melodies of the Peking Opera remain Erhuang and Xipi. Of the two, the music of the former is more graceful, sedate, lower, and slower, appropriate to rather serious circumstances, while the latter is more vivacious, quicker, and higher, suitable for more light-hearted occasions. The pitch of the bowed fiddle is tuned a tone lower for Erhuang music than for Xipi, which is why the former sounds lower than the latter. The rhythm of both melodies is based on simple time, that is, two or four beats to the bar, but several very quick rhythms are found in Xipi but not in Erhuang, validating the idea that the one is generally faster moving than the other.

Alterations in rhythm and musical texture give variety to these two melodies, but there are also a range of others used in Peking Opera. The influence of the elegant Kunqu, for instance, is quite substantial, and as a result some of the numerous melodies of that southern style have found their way into the Peking Opera.

The orchestra of the traditional Peking Opera is quite small. One of the most prominent instruments is a small drum, the *danpi*, whose player acts also as the orchestra conductor by setting the rhythm for the other musicians. Another instrument used for beating out the rhythm is the clapper, *ban*, which consists of two pieces of wood flicked against each other to produce a high woody clack (Figure 3.5). However, by far the most important instruments of the Peking Opera orchestra are the *huqin*, a class of two-string bowed fiddles, which includes the smaller *jinghu* and larger *jingerhu* (Figure 3.6). These instruments are so vital to the success of a performance that in the 1870s the

3.5 The conductor of the Peking Opera orchestra is the player of the small drum called *danpi*; he strikes the drum with his right hand while flicking the clapper with his left. Also shown here is a player of a *jinghu* fiddle.

practice arose for leading Peking Opera actors to hire their own private fiddle players to accompany them as they sang.

Other instruments in the Peking Opera orchestra include the plucked, round 'moon guitar', the *yueqin*, the plucked 'three string' or *sanxian* (Figure 3.7), and, in those items derived from Kunqu, the side-blown Chinese flute called the *dizi*. The *suona* is a double-reeded wind instrument, and although it is in this respect similar to an oboe, the reed is much smaller and the tone much shriller than for the Western instrument. Sometimes a *suona* phrase ends a scene, and, played to sound like whinnying, it symbolizes the riding of a horse. In battle scenes, the percussion play together noisily but without singing or melody, to symbolize fighting and conflict. Very occasionally total

3.6 The musician ahown here is playing the *jingerhu*, the larger Peking Opera fiddle.

3.7 A player of the three-string, plucked, low-pitched *sanxian* before a performance. A *pipa* lies behind him on the left.

silence prevails over an extended period, one example being the mime scene in *The Crossroads*, as the two main characters pretend an inability to see one another.

55

In the modern dramas and the *xinbian lishi ju*, the music retains the style of the traditional theatre, but it is by no means identical to it. In the Shanghai-produced dramas *Heir Apparent Exchanged for a Leopard Cat* and *Cao Cao and Yang Xiu*, the orchestra is quite large, sitting in a pit with a conductor in the Western style and not at the side of or on the stage, as is the case during most traditional items. It has not only the standard Chinese instruments but some Chinese and Western additions as well, including the Chinese four-string plucked lute, the *pipa* (Figure 3.8), and the Western double bass, cello, and flute. *Cao Cao and Yang Xiu* even has quite extensive passages written for the old Chinese seven-string zither, the *guqin*, an instrument popular with the educated élite but not ordinarily played in Peking Opera. The texture of the singing voices remains largely unchanged, but the sound as a whole is considerably more intense with the larger orchestra than in the purely traditional Peking Opera.

3.8 A player of the *pipa*, the Chinese lute. Although an important ilnstrument in many contexts, the *pipa* is not common in the traditional Peking Opera orchestra but has assumed greater importance for newly written items.

4

How is the Peking Opera
Doing Nowadays?

One of the most interesting developments in Chinese culture and society since the period of reform began in the late 1970s has been the simultaneous but contradictory thrust towards modernization on the one hand and the revival of traditions on the other. There is a strong tendency for older people, especially men, to welcome the traditional revival but for younger people to prefer those arts which they see as more relevant to the modern age. Although the distinction is far from clear-cut, the traditions are usually those of China, while the modern arts either come from or show very strong influences from the West.

For the Peking Opera, these trends have had somewhat contradictory effects. Traditional operas are available in performance, as sheet music and recordings, and through broadcasts, but many people are concerned about what significance they really hold in the modernizing China. The creative outburst in the early 1980s which produced many *xinbian lishi ju*, historical dramas written in the Peking Opera style, had dried up by the end of that decade.

The genre of the *xinbian lishi ju* was, in any case, not helped by the 4 June 1989 crack-down by the central authorities on the student movement. The newly written items tend to carry quite clear political implications, even though set in the past, and the crack-down made all artists far more cautious than they had been earlier about touching on political issues. It is fair to add that by 1992, however, this caution had to a large extent dissipated, with the result that creativity was to some degree restored.

As its name and history suggest, the centre for Peking Opera has traditionally been the capital, Beijing. In the 1990s, however, most of the new items being created come from centres other than Beijing itself. Tianjin, not far from Beijing, Shanghai, China's most populous city, Nanjing, the capital of Jiangsu province up the Yangtze River from the coast, and Wuhan, the Hubei capital in central China which sits quite a bit further up the Yangtze from Nanjing, are among the most important sources for new dramas. Beijing has tended recently to rely primarily on its traditional prestige, while the other centres have been more adventurous in their approach to the Peking Opera.

The only venue in Beijing which, as of the mid-1990s, still stages a Peking Opera performance every evening of the year is the Pear Garden Theatre (*Liyuan juchang*), founded in 1990, which is located within the Front Gate Hotel (*Qianmen fandian*) on Yongan lu (Eternal peace road). This hotel caters mainly to foreigners and consequently the audience at the Pear Garden Theatre is almost all from abroad, of course including Taiwanese and Hong Kong visitors and the patrons' associates from the PRC itself. Attendance is quite good and prices are very high by Chinese standards. It appears that the Beijing Municipal Peking Opera Company (*Beijingshi Jingju yuan*), which gives the performances, makes a great deal of money from the venture.

The content and setting of the Peking Opera performances in the Pear Garden Theatre are designed to be as traditional as possible. The items performed are all highly classical, and although there are modern appurtenances such as good and stable electric lighting, the aim is clearly to recreate the past as closely as possible and to strive for content which avoids anything reformed or modern. The structure of the theatre itself reflects nineteenth-century practices, which had the most expensive seats at the front, the audience sitting around comfortable tables, drinking tea, and eating nuts or fruit, although never a full dinner.

Another more genuine site is the Zhengyi Ci stage, mentioned in the previous chapter. This is actually a stage where performances are once again given after a long period of disuse. In this case there are attempts to revive not only the stage itself but also the customs among its patrons, such as the tables with tea and food provided. Again it is the Beijing Municipal Peking Opera Company which performs.

The best Peking Opera troupe in Beijing is the China Peking Opera Troupe (*Zhongguo Jingju yuan*). This group performs frequently, but generally it arranges to perform only for specific work units and not for the public at large. It does not normally sell tickets, except when a new opera is staged or during festivals. These festivals are held quite frequently, however, and occur especially at the time of holidays such as National Day, which falls on 1 October, or the Spring Festival, which is the equivalent of the lunar new year.

The performances at these festivals are of a very high standard and usually take place in the People's Theatre (*Renmin juchang*)(Plate 19), which is to the west of Beihai (North lake), on Huguosi lu (Protect the country temple street). Built in the 1950s, it is still the main theatre in contemporary style in Beijing for the mass performance of the Peking Opera, although it can be used for other purposes. The China Peking Opera Troupe performs there frequently. Although nowadays the city's newspapers advertise performances, the traditional practice of advertising outside the theatre is still followed. For instance, at a festival held in November 1995 to commemorate the fortieth anniversary of the establishment of the China Peking Opera Troupe, a signboard outside the People's Theatre announced

4.1 This signboard, outside the People's Theatre, announces the items to be performed for the 1995 festival in honour of the fortieth anniversary of the founding of the China Peking Opera Troupe.

all the individual pieces to be performed over the festival's ten evenings, together with a list of the artists, the dates, and the times (Figure 4.1).

These festivals gain enthusiastic support from audiences and government organizations. At those performances of the 1995 festival which I attended, the People's Theatre was completely filled. Moreover, although older people tended to dominate, there were many young people in the audience, some of them couples, others with young children, especially girls. The atmosphere of the performance retained the vibrancy of earlier times, with people shouting *hao* ('good') frequently and giving applause far more generously than is usually heard nowadays. Although the festival came under criticism from some quarters for being too traditional and not including newly written works, it certainly inspired a great deal of enthusiasm from others who attended it.

In the mid-1990s two opposite trends are in evidence in the Peking Opera, one pointing to a bleak future for this art, but the other showing a revival of sorts. Young people are still defecting from the Peking Opera in droves. Competition from other forms of entertainment is keen. When a foreign pop group comes to town, such as the Swedish group Roxette early in 1995, young people are prepared to pay large sums for tickets and demand is so great that there is difficulty in getting in. But not many are prepared to pay very much smaller amounts of money with comparatively little effort to see performances of their own traditional Peking Opera.

Most young people find the dominant traditionalism of the Peking Opera boring. The Cultural Revolution, when all traditional items were banned, broke the thread of appreciation which had persisted since the birth of the genre. It created a generation which both could not understand the Peking Opera and did not see the point in trying to understand it. At the present time the school curricula are so crowded that it is not possible to include enough of this traditional art in the national curricula to make a real difference to what the youth thinks and feels about it. In some parts of China, Peking Opera enthusiasts are trying to increase its presence in the schools, but the outlook for this strategy is not particularly bright.

Another issue is the influence of television. The electronic medium is widespread throughout China in the 1990s, especially in the cities which are the main Peking Opera centres. It is so easy to turn on the television, whereas to go to the opera most likely involves a bicycle or bus ride, which may be time-consuming and uncomfortable, especially in the cold seasons, making an unappealing alternative to a comfortable evening at home.

Peking Opera is still telecast regularly on television in Beijing and even more often in Tianjin. This is clearly an effort to keep it alive and to respond to some demand. But it is said that the people who watch it are just the same as those who might go to see the Peking Opera in the first place, predominantly older men and with a notable lack of young people.

There is another, and a bit more optimistic, side to this picture. In the first place it is possible that many people, especially men, become more interested in the opera as they grow older. In the early 1980s, when traditional drama came back in the wake of the condemnation of the Cultural Revolution, many enthusiasts complained that people in the audiences were virtually all aged over 40. In the mid-1990s, the cut-off age should have moved up by over ten years, but it has not. For instance, in an article on attempts to revive the Peking Opera, the English-language *China Daily* of 21 November 1995 complained that 'people who frequent the Peking Opera theatres are mostly over the age of 40', and my numerous observations in Beijing and elsewhere over the years confirm that the boundary age of about 40 has not moved very much.

It is also very clear that Peking Opera professionals and lovers, with strong government support, are determined not to let this art die. In 1990 there was considerable fanfare given to a festival of Peking Opera and other activities held to mark the second centenary of the entry of the Anhui companies into Beijing. Jiang Zemin, the General Secretary of the CCP, was among the senior leaders who attended the opening performance of the festival. On several occasions Jiang has expressed his strong support for the national arts, giving particular mention to the Peking Opera. In the 1990s the leader most directly associated with the arts is Li Ruihuan, a member of the CCP Politburo's Standing

Committee and thus one of the most powerful people in the country. In a major speech made on 10 January 1990 he emphasized the magnificence of Chinese tradition and signalled support for the preservation of the traditional theatre, including Peking Opera, as a valued part of China's cultural heritage.

In November 1995, the government of the Tianjin municipality, long a major centre for Peking Opera, expended a considerable sum of money to host the First Festival of Peking Opera Arts, which was designed specifically to bring about a revival in the fortunes of the genre. Li Ruihuan attended the opening session, which was an extravaganza telecast over Central Chinese Television. The festival included not only performances of new works, but also competitions and prizes.

In contrast to the festival at the People's Theatre in Beijing, this one laid emphasis on the newer *xinbian lishi ju*. Although the themes were mostly set in the distant past, the music and production style definitely showed some nontraditional and reformed features. For instance, in *Heir Apparent Exchanged for a Leopard Cat*, in the extended scene which ends with Kou Zhu's collapse and death, the torture was made as realistic and harrowing as possible, not left to the imagination as would most certainly have been the case in a more traditional performance.

There is a trend among certain young intellectuals to admire Peking Opera as representative of a kind of latter-day nationalism. One student expressed an opinion which may be quite widespread. She said that, although she herself rarely goes to see the Peking Opera and does not like it much, she will encourage her child to see and appreciate it as an important part of China's traditional cultural heritage.

In the period of reform, the Shanghai Peking Opera Company has taken the lead in encouraging university students to revive their interest in Peking Opera as a part of China's culture. They have staged excellent performances which are free or very cheap for students, and invited them to take part in discussions on ways to reform the Peking Opera. These attempts began in Shanghai in the early 1980s and in 1995 the company went to Beijing to spread its message in that city. This activity has produced quite an effect in Shanghai, although few would claim that it has been able to reassert the Peking Opera's vitality as an art form within society as a whole. A performance in the university section of Beijing in November 1995 was full, although not with standing-room only, and the audience was very responsive and enthusiastic.

Another aspect of this semi-revival is growth in the number of amateur groups (*piaofang*) in the 1990s. These are simply groups of Peking Opera enthusiasts who meet regularly to perform for each other. The city having the largest number is Tianjin, with about 150, but there are also some 100 in Beijing. One such Beijing group is the Society for the Research and Practice of the Arts of the Mei Lanfang School of Peking Opera (*Meipai yishu yanxi she*), founded in 1989 (Figure 4.2). Its members meet once a week, except in winter, to sing Peking Opera music in the style of Mei Lanfang. Most members are fairly old, both men and women, but there are some younger ones as well. Mei was a male performer of female roles, and both men and women amateurs sing his music enthusiastically.

There are still two schools of Peking Opera in Beijing. Their standards are high, and the qualifications of the children attending them is said to be showing a steady improvement. About 270 students were attending the Beijing Municipal Traditional Drama School (*Beijingshi xiqu xue-*

4.2 A meeting of the Beijing *piaofang* called the Society for the Research and Practice of the Arts of the Mei Lanfang School of Peking Opera.

xiao) in September 1995, a number somewhat less than in earlier days. Of these, about 60 per cent were boys, reflecting the demands placed by the casts of Peking operas. Although the school is still heavily subsidized by the state, fees were introduced in 1995 to help meet the growing costs. This development is very much in line with changes elsewhere in the educational system, which underwent heavy privatization processes in the 1990s.

Demand to enter the school is still considerable, with only about one in seven applicants being accepted annually. Criteria for entry include the results of an audition and evaluation of the candidate's physical appropriateness. (Even though China has recently begun moves to give disabled people a better deal, it is simply not feasible for them to become Peking Opera actors, because of the enormous physical demands of the art.) The course lasts seven years, and most students enter at about the age of twelve. The new students have already received some of the mainstream education, and the courses at the school include 'culture' courses. These consist of general material the same as in other schools, the aim being to prevent students from growing up with no skills other than those necessary for the Peking Opera.

A performance by the students of the school included sketches by two children aged about seven, one boy and one girl . Each of these had been accepted well below the normal age of entry because of the promise of great talent. The standards of all the students, not only these two, were absolutely superb . There is clearly no shortage of talent among young Chinese for Peking Opera acting and singing (Plates 20–22). This situation bodes well for future performance standards and is at least one reason for optimism that this great art will not die out in the foreseeable future, even if demand among Chinese audiences shrinks.

Efforts by the government and others to revive the Peking Opera should not dismissed out of hand. After all, governments have ways and means of helping or opposing the fortunes of an art form that can be decisive. What the Chinese government's activities, festivals, and major events cannot do, however, is to re-establish the strong link between the Peking Opera and the society at large. Peking Opera is no longer an art form relevant to the population. It does not push itself into the dreams of the people, and especially of the youth, in the way it once did. Representative of an era which is past and never to be restored, it is unlikely ever really to have such influence again. It will not necessarily die out—that also is most unlikely, at least within the next century. But its attraction will be as an example of the nation's important artistic heritage, not as truly representative of the styles and concerns of the current generation.

Like other regional styles of theatre in China, the Peking Opera is becoming an art form for the special occasion. There is no reason to doubt the quite genuine enthusiasm people feel for an occasion such as the First Festival of Peking Opera Arts. Not only was the opening session telecast live and in full, and the city festooned with banners lauding the festival and 'painted face' images, but conversations with ordinary people in Tianjin at the time left me with the strong impression that the event had sunk, with some pride, into the consciousness even of those people with little interest in Peking Opera. Moreover, the festival saw the performance of some truly excellent dramas. Once such an occasion is over, however, the residual enthusiasm may not be either strong or lasting.

The future of the Peking Opera may resemble that of a popular museum piece. This is not to decry it. Museums are more important in the present age than they have ever been. They are visited frequently and, just as elsewhere, teachers make it their business to take the children in their charge to admire the national cultural heritage. The arts of the past have their clientele and older people have as much right to their loves in the arts as do younger ones. But the heyday of the Peking Opera is over and the semi-revival of Peking Opera of the mid-1990s is unlikely to yield another similar flourishing.

Glossary

chou	a clown; characterized by a large white mark on and around the nose, he is usually a humorous or ridiculous character, but occasionally a villain
dan	a female role
danpi	a small drum, the player of which conducts the Peking Opera orchestra
dizi	the Chinese flute, a side-blown reedless wind instrument
guqin	a seven-string zither, ancient and aristocratic, used by scholars but never, until very recently, in the Peking Opera
huadan	'flower female role'; a vivacious and flirtatious woman
hualian	a 'painted face role'; the role category for which stylistic painting of the face is the dominant feature
huqin	two-string fiddle
jing	a 'painted face role'; the role category in which stylistic painting of the face is the dominant feature
laodan	'old female role'; old woman
laosheng	'old male role'; educated and dignified men, such as officials and emperors
mo	'supporting male role'; in the *nanxi*, this character introduced the story
nanxi	'southern drama'; the style of drama found in the south of China beginning in the twelfth century AD
piaofang	'amateur group'; an association of Peking Opera enthusiasts who meet regularly to perform for each other

pipa	the Chinese lute, a four-string plucked instrument
qingyi	literally meaning 'bluish clothes', this is the term for the primary female role, usually a demure and well-behaved young woman
sheng	a male role
shuixiu	literally 'water sleeve', this is the term for the very long sleeves which are an ancient part of some women's costumes
si da mingdan	'four great famous *dan*': Mei Lanfang, Cheng Yanqiu, Shang Xiaoyun, and Xun Huisheng
suona	the Chinese oboe, a double reeded, shrill-sounding wind instrument
wudan	'military female role'; a female fighter, skilled in the military arts
wusheng	'military male role'; generals, or any male characters who take part in battles
xiaosheng	'young male role'; the scholar-lover, the younger man of letters
xinbian lishi ju	'newly written historical dramas'; items which use material from before the modern period but rework it according to contemporary standards and rules
xinxi	'new plays'; dramas written by literary figures for specific actors, especially in the Republican period
yudai	'jade belt'; a circular belt worn with ceremonial robes
yueqin	the 'moon guitar', a plucked, four-string instrument with a spherical body

Selected Bibliography

Hsu Tao-ching, *The Chinese Conception of the Theatre*, Seattle: University of Washington Press, 1985.

Huang Shang, *Tales from Peking Opera*, Beijing: New World Press, 1985.

Mackerras, Colin, *Chinese Drama: A Historical Survey*, Beijing: New World Press, 1990.

Mackerras, Colin, *The Chinese Theatre in Modern Times from 1840 to the Present Day*, London: Thames and Hudson, 1975.

Mackerras, Colin, *The Rise of the Peking Opera 1770-1870: Social Aspects of the Theatre in Manchu China*, Oxford: Clarendon, 1972.

Pan Xiafeng, *The Stagecraft of Peking Opera: From Its Origins to the Present Day*, Beijing: New World Press, 1995.

Scott, A. C., *Actors Are Madmen: Notebook of a Theatregoer in China*, Madison: University of Wisconsin Press, 1982.

Scott, A. C., *Mei Lan-fang: Leader of the Pear Garden*, Hong Kong: Hong Kong University Press, 1959.

Scott, A. C., *The Classical Theatre of China*, London: George Allen & Unwin, 1957.

Wichmann, Elizabeth, *Listening to Theatre: The Aural Dimension of Beijing Opera*, Honolulu: University of Hawaii Press, 1991.

Wu Zuguang, Huang Zuolin, and Mei Shaowu, *Peking Opera and Mei Lanfang: A Guide to China's Traditional Theatre and the Art of its Great Master*, Beijing: New World Press, 1981.

Zhao Menglin and Yan Jiqing, with drawings by Zhao Menglin, *Peking Opera Painted Faces — with Notes on 200 Operas*, Beijing: Morning Glory Publishers, 1992.

Index

71

MAP OF CHINA